Creative Writing
Anthology **2011**

Poetry

egg b●x

UEA Creative Writing Anthology 2011

Poetry

First published by Egg Box Publishing, 2011

International © retained by individual authors

This book is sold subject to the condition that it shall not, by way of trade or otherwise, be lent, resold, hired out, stored in a retrieval system, or otherwise circulated without the publisher's prior consent in any form of binding or cover other than that in which it is published and without a similar condition including this condition being imposed on the subsequent purchaser.

A CIP record for this book is available from the British Library.

UEA Creative Writing Anthology 2011 is typeset in Oranda 11pt on 12.5pt Leading.

Printed and bound by:
The MPG Books Group,
Bodmin and King's Lynn

Designed and typeset by:
Kettle of Fish Design, Norwich
www.kettleoffishdesign.com

Proofed by:
Sarah Gooderson

Distributed by:
Central Books

ISBN:
978-0955939990

Acknowledgements

Thanks to the following for making this anthology possible:

The Malcolm Bradbury Memorial Fund, the Centre for Creative and Performing Arts at the University of East Anglia and The School of Literature & Creative Writing at UEA in partnership with Egg Box Publishing.

We'd also like to thank the following people:

Moniza Alvi, Trezza Azzopardi, Jean Boase-Beier, Amit Chaudhuri, Andrew Cowan, Giles Foden, Sarah Gooderson, Lavinia Greenlaw, Rachel Hore, Kathryn Hughes, Michael Lengsfield, Jean McNeil, Natalie Mitchell, Natalie Orr, Rob Ritchie, Michèle Roberts, Helen Smith, Henry Sutton, George Szirtes, Val Taylor and Rebecca Wigmore.

Nathan Hamilton at Egg Box Publishing and Catrin & Dylan Lloyd-Edwards at Kettle of Fish Design.

Editorial team:

Desmond Avery
Oonagh Barronwell
Dwight Dunston
Tamsin Flower
Anthony Good
Tom Graves
Edwin Kelly
Francesca Kletz
Eugene Noone
Maureen Phillips
Elizabeth Michelle Ruddick
Charlotte Stretch
Rouan Wilsenach

UEA Creative Writing Anthology 2011

Contents

Foreword
Moniza Alvi and George Szirtes i

Poetry
.... 10

Contributors
Rosie Breese 12
Dwight Dunston 24
Petra Kamula 34
Rouan Wilsenach 46

Interview with Alice Oswald 58

UEA Creative Writing Anthology 2011

Foreword

by **Moniza Alvi** and **George Szirtes**

The work of any single year in the Masters course depends on a coming together of different voices that develop in company with each other. There is no point in trying to hold young poets to a single standard of excellence. Excellence is achieved by listening, learning and experimenting: range is vital. This year too, among the mixture of full-time and part-time students (twelve altogether) we have seen a considerable range of poetics in development.

    The workshops lie at the core of the experience and a good group will make full use of the opportunities time and friendship offer. It is possible to see how one poet's idea moves in and out of the general discussion, leaving its traces, asking its questions as the work is debated intelligently, generously, and with an open mind. Being part of such a group, both as student and as tutor, is a privilege. Everyone learns, everyone moves at their own pace, everyone finds stimulus in this or other area, at this or other time. It is, necessarily, an intense time and brief. Within a year students produce some thirty-nine poems, a good way to a collection, but the poems are not static. They are revised, discarded, reworked, turn into other poems. Few people write in quite the same way at the end as they did at the beginning.

    As regards this year, although students have been inspired by each other's writing, it has often been the sheer energy of the work that has transferred itself and played a part in the strengthening of the individuality of each poet.

Students have developed that sixth sense of discovering in their reading that which will be most useful to their development. It is this wide reading, and also the performances and talks given by this year's visiting writers, David Harsent, Alice Oswald and Jo Shapcott, which have enriched the course and provided the necessary, bracing 'outside air'.

The poems have been stylistically extremely adventurous and it has been a delight to witness each poet stretching the bounds of what language can achieve. All the more a delight as the poems have not been mere exercises, but have carried the force of those that had to be written.

While the intensity of the course has been a real, sometimes almost overwhelming challenge, its rewards include the poets' accelerated development in the company of those who are passionate about poetry.

And so on to the individual contributors.

Dwight Dunston is an American poet. His work depends on distillation and understatement. There is a strong sense of personal and moral forces acting on the imagination – there is a suggestion of right and wrong action, as in 'The Crash' – but they are lightly applied, heard almost as a white background noise, or felt as a mild but steady breeze. The short poems here are like the title of one of his poems, 'The breath before the abdomen tightens'. There the soul is lost, but its loss is not presented as a grand or spectacular event. There is instead a steadiness, then silence. Another short poem, 'On Going to a Private School', presents in four lines a complexity that has been concentrated towards one clear firm and troubling statement. It is the apparent simplicity of articulation that lends poems like 'Honey' their power.

One can get an idea of the range of work this year by looking at Rosie Breese's collection of poems. The pace here is very different from Dunston's, an intense staccato, as in the sequence 'Edges' which, as the 'Razor' section tells, is 'to pulse something of self'. That pulse beats through a series of vignettes or notations, each a kind of sharpness. There is experimentation with typographic devices and spacing, as in 'Glyphs', and in the playful Edwin Morganesque, 'lighten our darkness ... ', though the play here has a proper sense of desperation. Even the poems that register objective experience, such as 'light on the river', will look to 'clench like quick fists, / gather / the sun that breaks / itself over water' as the poet puts it. The last poem, 'No more talk', returns us to the edges with a beautifully realised single sentence that ends in an exclamation, a simple 'Oh'.

Working in sequences, in which a multitude of ideas are given space to breathe and resonate, has been enabling for the Australian poet, Petra Kamula. She has been influenced by Selima Hill, but the visceral images and their inventive development are her own. In 'Night Ward' she creates a vigorous metaphoric chain where toes are 'white minnows / or sperm or phosphorescence // reflected in a drunk sailor's eyes / before he tumbles into depth.' The bold poem 'Weigh In' leaps lightly from crocodile swamps to the 'Dance of the Sugar Plum Fairy', riding on a wave of inspiration. She is unafraid of the large gesture: 'I am the sky after birds have abandoned it', and she revels in apt word-play as in the eating disorder sequence where the young woman is 'grasping, snouting / an-nor-rex – like a King!' Through the drama of poems in which personae such as the butcher's and the fishmonger's daughters speak, she explores other voices, thus extending her own.

Rouan Wilsenach's poetry often concerns the storying through which we make sense of our lives, particularly the stories of the land, of his homeland South Africa. His recent poems have developed an impressively rich narrative texture. The wealth of stories of Johannesburg become the subject of an urgent quest: 'Are they settled in the cavernous belly / below the surface, have they been / mined out, sifted through, discarded / for their poor

Foreword

trade value?' The land is animated, personified, its significance heightened: a dam waits for water 'like a barren ghost / for children to arrive', the hospitable mulberry tree of childhood 'adopts us, / welcomes us into her branches / with a creak'. As well as the relationship to place, human relationships also feature in this selection. 'Close to the end' achieves a grounded, yet mythic quality, as the couple examines books with their endings ripped out, and everything around them 'becomes imbued with fiction'.

The beauty of poetry, if one may use a word like *beauty* without embarrassment at dragging a word with such a heavy baggage of association into the discussion, lies in the peculiar living relationship a poet forms with language. Each poem is a sense of life: the way that life works itself through language. Language has dimensions. It has history, colour, music, argument, currency, weight, mystery. It is the air the consciousness of the poet inhabits. The poet is not, however, a specially blessed or cursed being, but a person like you and me, a kind of specialist Everyman / Everywoman trying to make difficult, tense beauty out of a difficult shifting sense of life. When the poem arrives its beauty appears simple in its own terms. But that simplicity is the product of those complex dimensions. Here are the dimensions and those difficult simplicities, in movement as it were. Works in progress, as all works are.

Can writing poetry be taught? One might debate whether 'taught' is the right word, but there is certainly much to learn and much that can be fostered. An MA course at a significant point in a poet's development provides a structure, the boundaries within which adventures in writing can take place, and it is hoped, a life-long point of reference.

We are extremely grateful to Alice Oswald who kindly agreed to answer some questions put in email form by students (and staff) following her visit.

MA and GS

UEA Creative Writing Anthology 2011

Poetry

Rosie Breese
Dwight Dunston
Petra Kamula
Rouan Wilsenach

Rosie Breese

Edges
The rise and fall of Lawnchair Larry
lighten our darkness we beseech thee o lord
Glyphs
light on the river
rorschach
No more talk

Edges

Skin I

Gauze skims a ghost
unmattered   unwoken

between night sweats and light
a body   unbordered

Razor

It is Bic to paper, living story.
It is not to die. It is to pulse
something of self, of my red self raining,
materialising like a wish.
It is cave painting, outlasting thousands.
It is not not. It is is.

Gas

Apply click to hiss.
Blue eye widens:

ability of skin
to crater, bacon-smelling –

to be outside as in,
branded Zero.

Scissors

Legs ratchet open for birth
of skin below skin, the true skin, unhardened.

Fat cells wink sheepish; crown through red ripple.
I know them. I know them. They know who I am.

Steam

Baby's breath
edgeless

until I hold out a hand,

see cloud colour me
a rising sun.

Door

What if it   open   should blue   my eye socket

What is it   the outside   the view from a bruise

Skin II

My jumper shifts, lights feverish scabs
a healthy pink like dawn. I'm glowing
in the darkest places

I am   lit up

against suck of mud, against greywash of pavement,
against air, its wavering uncommitment.
It takes this, but I know my edges.

The rise and fall of Lawnchair Larry

In the 'Inspiration', a patio chair tied to helium-filled weather balloons, Larry Walters inadvertently rose to a height of 15,000 feet and drifted into federal airspace before crash-landing into power lines, gaining overnight fame in the process. He later committed suicide in Angeles National Forest.

The *Inspiration* scuds me through emptiness.
Silence volleys up on the thermals, bears me
creaking on plastic slats. I realise now
I have trusted my life to hope and knotwork.
Strange. I always thought this would feel weightless.

Blue light collapses, ribboning red. Down there,
guys like me will be dreaming with the view,
will have it in their crosshairs, will have mapped
their invisible territories. Even here,
I drift into someone else's flight path. It seems

so much depends. My boots dangle, huge,
over cities stacked high with hearts and heads.
Even here, a man can't just sit around.
I crack a beer. The cap spins, glinting, to earth.

*

Circuit-board city winking to blackout.
Power lines have made a resistor of me.
Tonight, we will rediscover candlelight,
see how all that we love can flicker.

Forest of faces. Another dinner,
another tall tale. I'm inflated
to bursting. You know, so much depends
on the story. Beginning, flight, and then ...

The *Inspiration* sags in a garage,
its sandbags dribbling. Time is running out.
This body suddenly lacking ballast,
called forever upwards. We all have to try

our limits. This sky, just a balloon's span
bullet-holed. The sun reaching through.

```
l i g h t e n     o u r      d a r k n e s s      w e      b e s e e c h      t h e e      o    l o r d
                              d a r k n e s s       w e                 h                  o    l       d
                              a                          b                                  t    o    l       d
            h     e           a r                                        t
            h     e        r              e                              t
   i        t
   i
   i           n                          s         w                                       o           r d
   i           n              a r                                        t

               n    o
            t e               a r          s                        h                       o    l       d
                     u                         s                                                 l       d
   i           n    o
       h                      a r   n e s s             e s

               n    o
      g h           o                      s                             t
         h          o                      s                             t
            t       o
               e              a                                          t

                              a            s     w e
            t e                                  s                       t
               n                           e     w
  l i          n                           e s
                    o                n                                             o   l       d
                                                 w                                 o       o   d
  l            e                                                         t
                     u                     s                 b e
                              d a r k n e s s
                                                 w e            s e e
               n    o
  l           e                            s s
  l i g h t
```

Glyphs

This is CAPITAL CITY: a gridlock in monospace.
Here the acronyms flourish,
superstructures unLtd. Their double-glazed stems
stretch into God's old quarters.

Our universities have no time for etymology.
Even the stones have forgotten their names
and so, cry nothing.

Past versions are overmatter, burning brightly out
as the body sleeps. Their voices have driven thousands mad.

Our advice is the same for everyone.
Leave only your footprints at the margins.
There is nowhere to go but around
and nothing to be but subscript,

although on a clear night you might look up, watch
                              the glyp h s   d r i f t.

light on the river

dog in the water, caught
in rejoicing of muscle,
music of shards

mirrorball surface turns on undertow,
scatters sky's gift:
confetti of light

pupils clench like quick fists,
gather
the sun that breaks
itself over water

creatures held ecstatic
in outlines split open

rorschach

one evening he fell asleep
brush in hand   I stole it

dipped it   red and wet   painted
on his chest   my heart   waking him

he pulled me close   we rolled and blurred
the heart mirrored   a rorschach test

did we see this   the blood between us
spread thin and drying

No more talk

This sentence:
a trail of full stops
sputtering from the sky's wire,
ticking into the telephone's gullet,
its moulded lips still mouthing Oh.

Rosie Breese was born in 1983 and grew up in the 1850s. She is currently based in Cambridge, where she works as an English teacher. Her work has previously appeared in *nthposition*, *3:AM Magazine*, *Agenda* and *Poetry Wales*. She has never seen *Star Wars*, and has no desire to.

Dwight Dunston

Hamstring
Honey
The Crash
These Precious Lives
On Going to a Private School
The breath before the abdomen tightens
On a stranger telling a mother she has lost her child
The Leaf and the Sky
Dreaming of Stones

Hamstring

You can hear the body shred
when it happens.

The fibers quickly unfasten
and refuse to zip.
Scar tissue begins to knot.

There is no time for preparation.
Anticipation would only ruin you.
(Recall the flailing tooth your dad snatched from your mouth.)

Long after, you will forget the pain,
forget the sight of your tooth hanging by a string,
the smell of ointment pressed to myalgia.

But the sound of shredding will be familiar soon.
Not knowing if it will be fast or slow
will rot you until then.

Honey

You were the honey in the jar
as well as the bread it is drizzled on
to sweeten the taste.

Which means
you were an excess
but necessary.

And in removing you
I learned
to have the simplest hunger.

To be unhappy but breathing,
naked but cool,
estranged but at peace.

Still I wonder
if the space you have left
can be filled

and if not,
how to rid the days
of your sweetness.

The Crash

And was it wrong for me
to talk to you about the future
as if we would both be there?
Could anyone call us bold
for being young and making plans
for our young age?
Perhaps I should've been silent,
keeping the future at arm's length,
letting it come to us slowly
from our blindside.
From your blindside.
It would crash into us, surely,
but it would've been minor.
"I" would've survived.

But instead,
being the boy I was,
I forced us to take it head on.
And when the future

removed your fiber
from its fine robe,

I had to gather up the strength
to look away
from the empty seat next to me
and focus
on the gaping distance

as it looked straight back
as if to sing its own praises and ask
So, what are you planning to do now?

These Precious Lives

They say blood is the most precious mineral there is
and soon it will be harvested.

Do ruby lives ruined
make rubied hands?

Yes

So, everything would be precious?

So precious.

On Going to a Private School

And it wasn't their color
but what colored them that was different.

And it was the empty part of their eyes

that emptied the color in me.

The breath before the abdomen tightens

is the eternal moment before the preacher resumes
when the soul listens for sound to steer it
        from being lost
                      but is lost.

On a stranger telling a mother she has lost her child

Say whatever you like to console her,
but none of it will be heard
after the worst.

Unless you can tell her exactly
where her child has gone,

but then, Lord knows, you would be her saviour
not a stranger.

The Leaf and the Sky

Each year the leaf, so young,
grows old
in its trial to reach the sky.

The sky stares down
and helplessly watches
the struggling flake.

As the months turn
and the green bends to brown,
the leaf grows too heavy to hold itself.

In falling, the wind provides
one last chance
for the leaf to sip the sky.

The closest the two
have ever been
before.

Dreaming of Stones

The stones are soft today,
smooth under my feet
as I stroll along the beach
towards the place you last stood
before you walked into the water.
No, I wasn't there,
nor do I know if there were stones on the beach,
or a beach for that matter.
Maybe the sea stretched right to your bedside
so you had no choice but to walk into it.
Yes, that is how it happened,
at least that is what will happen today.
Tomorrow, I'll dream that you walked
miles just to reach the shore,
feet too tired to walk you back
so you rested, forever.

Dwight Sterling Dunston was born in Philadelphia, PA and graduated from Dickinson College in 2010 where he studied English and Creative Writing. His passion for writing stems from his desire to make sense of the events that make our lives unique and intertwined, all at once.

Petra Kamula

The Butcher's Daughter
The Butcher's Daughter At 15
The Fishmonger's Daughter
Metamorphosis:
    Red Bucket Heart
    Afternoon Tea In Our Rooms
    I Transform Into A Skyscraper
    I Transform Into A Scalpel
    More Delicious Than Anything
    Night Ward
    Weigh In
    In The Garden After Weigh In

The Butcher's Daughter

I wake early, begin before the sun
tips itself red onto my hands.

Hush, hush. I've learnt the songs I must sing
to the heifers and their calves. I'm already

well acquainted with blood.
Clots and stains as thick as tongues.

I carry it in cups.
I put my mouth to their warm flanks.

Smell the shudder of sweat that comes
hot in the moments before death,

how it bounces back from my night-bare skin
and the hard press of the clay floor.

The Butcher's Daughter At 15

I turn a bright light over my nakedness,
pull the reluctant grey curtains to, heavy as hides.

I hold a mirror below me
as if I am stepping from it like Botticelli's Venus;

squat and spread myself open – see – see
what I have already come to know:

slippery oyster fins,
flushed ears and rubied cheeks –

aliveness of fresh meat.

The Fishmonger's Daughter

I do not like the butcher's daughter
who is full and ripe as a rotten egg near to bursting.

Her thighs shaped like legs of beef or ham, jamon
jamon the foreigners say, turning a piece of cured flesh

into something that shudders to life
with a muscular beauty.

Metamorphosis

(a partial sequence)

Note: The following eight poems are written in the voice of a young woman during her time at a live-in eating disorder clinic.

Red Bucket Heart

I stand in front of the mirror and tear everything away –
all the layers of my skin, the eyes

are easy to clip and pop-socket,
the plush of lips

I unhook, the flute of larynx
I pare away, the reeds of ribs

and the sharp bones of the foot
lift up like tiny helicopters,

the ligaments, lobes of fat, lamp lungs,
they all come away.

I even rip out my red bucket heart
with its antennae of valves and arteries

and those cave-like chambers
big enough, they say, to house
the echoes of love.

Afternoon Tea In Our Rooms

Wobbling on trays like wind-up toys
the dessert comes in large porcelain cups

creamy as our mothers' breasts
made firm and new again;

the raisins on top are pointed black nipples
winking their little eyes at us.

I Transform Into A Skyscraper

    Reach up
    tip top toe
    stretch just
    a little more
  extend the fingers
  scratch at the stars.
Must I be the woman
  I was always told
    I could be?

    They said
     be twig
     be taut
   be an open
  window, or be
   a reflection.
  The buttresses
   steel my spine.
When people stop me
 I must bring to bear
  my great height
   and weight.

I Transform Into A Scalpel

I run my tongue over slick edges,
find my teeth, and find
desire. Go hunting for a corpse
and nestle myself inside. Sharpen
my mind.
          Sing a high pitch.

More Delicious Than Anything

It doesn't eat her
she eats it –
devours it, stuffs it
handful after handful
with glee, past her teeth
greedy for it
grasping, snouting
an – nor – rex – like a King!

Night Ward

I live in a world without mirrors
so I have no face, only hands.

The head does not exist.
I am trunk, I am trunc

ated and I dance carefully
with a sodden sort of bliss.

My toes are exceedingly beautiful.
I curl them

in on themselves, like a perfect shell, a fox paw,
or around Lucy's spike of a shoulder;

Anna's sly left knee; the handle
of Nurse's favourite tea-stained mug.

In the night my toes detach themselves
and swim about the corridors: white minnows
or sperm or phosphorescence

reflected in a drunk sailor's eyes
before he tumbles into depth.

When they curl back into me I sigh,
and I sigh, and we paddle out together

into dreams of men with heads
as big as houses.

Weigh In

You cannot record my weight. Let me explain.
I am a ghost

who wanders through humid swamps
chock full of salubrious crocodiles

whistling Dance of the Sugar Plum Fairy.
I march through the yellow dust of the road

with a line of beheaded soldiers whose eyes
bead at me from the rolls of their dumpy knapsacks.

I am an infection, prised from within myself by the Doctor,
his slippery pincers click clacking.

He questions the translucency of my flesh,
prescribes me a chemical wash and says

'draw me a portrait of your soul'.
So I divide myself into exact eighths

and draw the sashimi jellyfish of my body.
I want someone to take hold of me

the way a surgeon caresses a frigid donor heart
softly, cooing to it 'little heart, pink up, pink up'.

I am the sky after birds have abandoned it
I am the sky as it grows arms

I am the sky as it climbs down
and finally rests its new feet

against the curved spine of the planet.

In The Garden After Weigh In
after Yehuda Amichai

I saw three women meet
and slowly devour each other
in the heat of a humid afternoon.
One was fair and stretched long as if a snake
had entered her at a young age
and whispered to her: stretch stretch;
one was dark and blood blistered
about all her parts and stuffed full
of plums and other bruised fruit
lushly overripe;
                     and then there was me
I ate myself with cheese
and with relishhhhhh!

And as we lay within
each others' rounded peach-stone bellies,
we pressed our faces into the skin of the world
and made small nose and elbow-shaped craters
and the earth became great in its rage
to fit so many people within its skin.

Petra Kamula was named after a boat, rather than the city. She is from Sydney, Australia. Her love of exploration and ancient history has seen her travel widely through Asia, Europe, North America and the Middle East. She writes poetry and short fiction, and is working on a novel.

Rouan Wilsenach

View from Buffelskop
Dust
Drought
Johannesburg
Mulberry stains
Tannin
Nocturne
Close to the end
In the dark

View from Buffelskop

> 'We have so long forgotten how to be intimate
> with immensity'
> **Anne Michaels**

Roads and rivers are thin veins
on the surface of a broad brown thigh.

The trees that I took shelter under on my way up
are flattened to splashes of paint.

My body refuses to accept what I see.
More terrain than it has sweat to imagine, let alone traverse.

The wind pushes at me in bursts like an excited child.
There is no room for thought up here.

I'm transfixed by this flat, brown body –
I trace its contours to the horizon

where it drops into blue
like a crocodile slipping into water.

My body is a pebble on this mountain,
immersed in endless sky.

[Buffelskop is a mountain in the Eastern Cape of South Africa]

Rouan Wilsenach

Dust

In Ireland, the poet says,
memory is amassed in mud.
Layers and layers of it,
wet and deep with history.
The Karoo is mudless, dry.

Dust is a poor storyteller,
she's forgetful, gets carried away
by the wind. Without substance,
she's impossible to hold. At night
she sneaks away while you ache
for stories. She's restless, indecisive,
dancing in the air, sleeping on the ground.

She reddens your eyes but steals
your tears. When it rains, each drop
browns her with moisture,
with the burden of memory
for a single moment,
before she shrugs it off in the heat.

[The Karoo is a semi-desert region in South Africa]

Drought

A windpump creaks to life
like a coffin lid lifting.
Metal bones, dancing in the wind.

The pump rod, a slender arm,
pulls and punches at the earth,
draws water
from deep under the modest folds
of her dry smitsvinger dress.

A trickle of water steadies,
pours from a black pipe,
splashes into the dam below,
which waits like a barren ghost
for children to arrive.

[Smitsvinger is a type of grass]

Johannesburg

This is dustland. The plateau,
hollowed years ago for gold, creaks
under the weight of busy lives
crammed into tin shacks, homes
piled together from scrap metal,
ready to join the dust in the wind.

Where are the stories of the dustland?
Are they settled in the cavernous belly
below the surface, have they been
mined out, sifted through, discarded
for their poor trade value? Do they lie
in towering heaps of fine sand
on the horizon, silhouetted in the sun?

Where are the stories?
Do they lie forgotten in the dust?
Do they paint the farmer's bakkie brown,
settle in the strands of children's hair,
on their school shoes as they walk
home from class? Are they forever waiting
to be stolen by the wind?

Where are its stories?
Are they drowned out by the crack
and roll of thunder, drenched in summer
downpours, washed away in torrents
along with bedding and clothes,
do they drift into dongas and die there,
sputtering for air, covered in mud?

The stories.
Do they warm and comfort the roots

of the jacaranda tree, where she stands,
alien to this land, in shallow soil
between the squatter camp and the road,
weeping her purple blossoms
onto the dusty sidewalk below?
Dustland.

[A bakkie is a pickup truck; a donga is a ditch caused by
 soil erosion]

Mulberry stains

In our old T-shirts, dotted with stains,
we set about climbing the mulberry tree.
She's not a big tree, wavers a bit
under the strain of our weight,
but we're children. She adopts us,
welcomes us into her branches
with a creak. We pick her fruit,
eat more than we harvest, pop
them into our gap-tooth mouths,
squish them between our fingers.

And while we're snug in bed
the mulberry tree rocks back and forth
in the gentle wind. The few overripe
berries we didn't pick, or those loosened
by our mischief, drop from her arms.
Some fall on the lawn, sink
between blades of grass to be absorbed
by the earth. Others stain the patio
with dark red pools
that blacken over the years.

Tannin

> *A bitter chemical released by some African thorn trees to*
> *make their leaves less appealing to browsing animals.*

An acacia leaf turns bitter
in my mouth. Its acrid taste
turns chewing into teaching,
etches tannin arcs into the rough
cracks on my tongue, a lesson
in licking another's wounds.

My grandfather smiles at me,
observing my reaction. He knows
the taste well, recognises the tug
I feel on the inside of my cheeks.

His sense of taste has left him,
he sends me to find him lemon juice
to see if it can bring his tongue
back to life. Even bitterness will do.

He tells me again about succulents
near the Karoo, how they haven't
developed this thorn-tree defence,
how kudus thrive there, browse
these sweet plants. I feed him
another ice cube to cool his drying mouth.

[A kudu is a species of antelope]

Nocturne

> '*I tell my piano the things I used to tell you.*'
> **Frédéric Chopin**

You find a scratched vinyl in the basement,
its label is nothing but a yellowed strip –
I watch you touch the needle to its surface,
your eyes narrowing as you listen to the static
for a trace of melody. For what feels
like hours we don't move, willing the crackle
to sing. I see your lips part, feel the air
you draw in as you hear the first note
break through. Muffled at first, like a voice
from behind a wall, the pianist plays
against the static tide. You smile
when you recognise it, raise
your hands above your knees and play
imaginary keys, your back arced.

Close to the end

None of these books have endings –
the last few pages are ripped out.
The two of us read them anyway,
imagine what's missing,
invent our own conclusions.

Stories are all we talk about.
Slowly, to pass the time. We share
our endings, compare the fates
we create. Everything around us
becomes imbued with fiction.

This room is cold, filled
floor to ceiling with beginnings.
We have a bottle of red wine
to keep us warm. We touch
the rough strip left behind

between the back cover and a page
that ends on half a sentence.
We run our fingers along the torn edge.
With closed eyes we feel the place
where endings once happened.

In the dark

There is no ocean.
We scoop salty sand
from this dry trench floor,
sprinkle it over our food for flavour.

But of course we have no food.
We close our eyes and grind
imagination between our teeth.

Not that closed eyes make any difference.
The sun's been gone too long.
We feel around for each other in the dark,
listen for the rustling of papery skin,

anything that may hint to us
that we are an *us* at all.

Rouan Wilsenach is from Johannesburg, South Africa. He studied Computer Science and English at Rhodes University. He worked as a software developer, before he was awarded a Commonwealth Scholarship to study at UEA. His poems have appeared in magazines in South Africa and the UK, including *New Coin*, *LitNet*, *Albatross* and *Orbis*.

UEA Creative Writing Anthology 2011

Alice Oswald Interview

Alice Oswald's collections include *Dart*, which won the T. S. Eliot Prize in 2002 and *Woods etc.* Her recent work includes *A Sleepwalk on the Severn* and *Weeds and Wild Flowers*, a collaboration with the artist **Jessica Greenman**.

In March 2011, **Alice Oswald** visited UEA as part of the university's Spring Literary Festival. She was interviewed onstage by **George Szirtes** and performed a memorable reading of her work. She has been kind enough to answer some further questions put to her by the four poets featured in this anthology and their tutors, **George Szirtes** and **Moniza Alvi**.

Rosie: Do you feel that your poems come from you, or to you – is the poem a pre-existing thing that needs to be 'felt' or 'heard' first, or is it entirely generated by the writer?

Alice: The finished poem is always slightly out of earshot, but earshot extends inwards as well as outwards, so I can't be sure whether it's a lost self speaking or something quite different and elsewhere.

Dwight: Do you feel that your poetry stems from a need to answer a question that you have posed to yourself?

Alice: Most visible, audible, tangible things radiate the question 'can you hear me?' to which I normally respond 'who are you?' and out of that cross-fire a poem might appear. But it doesn't leave me much time to ask *myself* any questions, except formal ones about metre etc.

Petra: How important are the classical stories and texts to your writing? How does that enrich what you write and feed into the tradition of what you write?

Alice: Classical characters are alive to me and when it's appropriate I consult them, though I know they are flighty. (The ones who helped me translate Homer left abruptly before I'd had time to edit.) I'm wary of the classical tradition and respond much more to archaic Greek, particularly the syntax of Homer.

Rouan: In many of your poems, natural objects such as flowers and stones become characters that reflect our own characteristics as humans. What attracts you to this kind of writing?

Alice: I don't see it as a 'kind of writing', more a way of life. All day long I rely on these things as close companions. I love the myopia of the natural world – the way a stone can only see you as a stone, a tree can only see you as a tree etc. It means you don't always have to be human.

Rosie: What do you feel is the value of the rise in university creative writing courses?

Alice: At worst it might produce a generation of brilliant readers, at best it might change the structure of literature into something more spreading and experimental.

George: Do you think there is such a thing as 'the life of a poet' in terms of what a young poet might do day to day, such as reading or activity or silence? How does it work for you?

Alice: I don't think anyone can second-guess what will impress the Muse. Sometimes she favours crime, sometimes she hangs out with librarians. The practical questions are more important: wage, house, clear head – for which gardening is one answer. Motherhood can provide friction, frustration, delight, anxiety, astonishment – all of which are helpful. Even unemployment would be OK. I suppose the only essential thing is to keep the imagination alive.

Dwight: How do you find power and meaning behind your own voice? Was there ever a time when you thought your voice and own ideas weren't quite ready to be expressed via poetry, or that poetry may not be the means to express your ideas?

Alice: I often have to wait a long time for power and meaning. When I write bad poems I quickly feel nauseous, but I do know that there are no other options for me – my prose is hopeless.

Rouan: As a reader, I find that your poems often take surprising turns. Do they sometimes surprise you while you are writing them?

Alice: Yes, I don't trust the *will* when I'm writing, which means I can't ever dictate how a poem will end. Between every phrase of a poem, there's a pause, into which, if you wait long enough, something from miles and miles away can enter.

Moniza: You are such a compelling reader of your poetry. I wonder if you have any advice or thoughts you could pass on to anyone just starting to read their work in public and feeling nervous about doing so?

Alice: The reading begins in the writing. I love true iambic pentameter, but 'freed' iambics have to me a very weak sound. If I'm not using formal meter, I steal the tunes of stressed verse – they lock the language in much tighter. I only read poems that I urgently want to speak and I think twice before reading anything ironic or unemphatic.